I0482990

This informational booklet provides a general overview of a particular topic related to OSHA standards. It does not alter or determine compliance responsibilities in OSHA standards or the *Occupational Safety and Health Act of 1970*. Because interpretations and enforcement policy may change over time, you should consult current OSHA administrative interpretations and decisions by the Occupational Safety and Health Review Commission and the Courts for additional guidance on OSHA compliance requirements.

This information is available to sensory impaired individuals upon request. Voice phone: (202) 693-1999; teletypewriter (TTY) number: (877) 889-5627.

www.osha.gov

Model Plans and Programs for the OSHA Bloodborne Pathogens and Hazard Communications Standards

U.S. Department of Labor
Elaine L. Chao, Secretary

Occupational Safety and Health Administration
John L. Henshaw, Assistant Secretary

OSHA 3186-06N
2003

Contents

Introduction

The mission of the Occupational Health and Safety Administration (OSHA) is to save lives, prevent injuries, and protect the health of America's workers. As part of the Department of Labor, OSHA promotes worker safety and health in every workplace in the United States.

OSHA'S bloodborne pathogens standard protects employees who work in occupations where they are at risk of exposure to blood or other potentially infectious materials. OSHA's hazard communication standard protects employees who may be exposed to hazardous chemicals. Both standards require employers to develop written documents to explain how they will implement each standard, provide training to employees, and protect the health and safety of their workers.

This publication includes a model exposure control plan to meet the requirements of the OSHA bloodborne pathogens standard and a model hazard communication program to meet the requirements of the hazard communication standard. The full text of these two OSHA standards, including the requirement for the written documents, is found in 29 CFR 1910.1030 and 29 CFR 1910.1200, respectively. You can access the full text of these standards through the OSHA website (www.osha.gov) by using the alphabetical index (click on "B" for the bloodborne pathogen standard; click on "H" for the hazard communication standard).

These model documents can be used as templates for your own workplace exposure control plan and hazard communication program, but you must tailor them to the specific requirements of your establishment. These sample plans contain all elements required by the bloodborne pathogens and hazard communication standards, so you should not eliminate any items when converting them for your own use. Your written plans must be accessible to all employees, either on-line or in an area where they are available for review on all shifts.

This publication provides general guidance on preparing written plans required by OSHA standards, but should not be considered a definitive interpretation for compliance with OSHA requirements. The reader should consult the OSHA bloodborne pathogens and hazard communication standards in their entirety for specific compliance requirements.

Part 1 Bloodborne Pathogens Standard

The following model for an Exposure Control Plan includes all elements required by the OSHA bloodborne pathogens standard (29 CFR 1910.1030). The intent of this model is to provide employers with an easy-to-use format that may be used as a template to develop a written exposure control plan tailored to the individual requirements of their establishments.

Model Exposure Control Plan

POLICY

The (Your facility name) is committed to providing a safe and healthful work environment for our entire staff. In pursuit of this goal, the following exposure control plan (ECP) is provided to eliminate or minimize occupational exposure to bloodborne pathogens in accordance with OSHA standard 29 *CFR* 1910.1030, "Occupational Exposure to Bloodborne Pathogens."

The ECP is a key document to assist our organization in implementing and ensuring compliance with the standard, thereby protecting our employees. This ECP includes:

- Determination of employee exposure

- Implementation of various methods of exposure control, including:
  Universal precautions
  Engineering and work practice controls
  Personal protective equipment
  Housekeeping

- Hepatitis B vaccination

- Post-exposure evaluation and follow-up

- Communication of hazards to employees and training

- Recordkeeping

- Procedures for evaluating circumstances surrounding exposure incidents

Implementation methods for these elements of the standard are discussed in the subsequent pages of this ECP.

PROGRAM ADMINISTRATION

- (Name of responsible person or department) is (are) responsible for implementation of the ECP. (Name of responsible person or department) will maintain, review, and update the ECP at least annually, and whenever necessary to include new or modified tasks and procedures. Contact location/phone number: _____ .

- Those employees who are determined to have occupational exposure to blood or other potentially infectious materials (OPIM) must comply with the procedures and work practices outlined in this ECP.

- (Name of responsible person or department) will provide and maintain all necessary personal protective equipment (PPE), engineering controls (e.g., sharps containers), labels, and red bags as required by the standard. (Name of responsible person or department will ensure that adequate supplies of the aforementioned equipment are available in the appropriate sizes. Contact location/phone number: _____.

- (Name of responsible person or department) will be responsible for ensuring that all medical actions required by the standard are performed and that appropriate employee health and OSHA records are maintained. Contact location/phone number: _____.

- (Name of responsible person or department) will be responsible for training, documentation of training, and making the written ECP available to employees, OSHA, and NIOSH representatives. Contact location/phone number: _____.

EMPLOYEE EXPOSURE DETERMINATION

The following is a list of all job classifications at our establishment in which all employees have occupational exposure:

Job Title	Department/Location
(Example: Phlebotomists)	(Clinical Lab)
(use as many lines as necessary)	

The following is a list of job classifications in which some employees at our establishment have occupational exposure. Included is a list of tasks and procedures, or groups of closely related tasks and procedures, in which occupational exposure may occur for these individuals:

Example:

Job Title   *Department/Location*   *Task/Procedure*

Housekeeper   Environmental Services   Handling Regulated Waste

(use as many lines as necessary)

NOTE: Part-time, temporary, contract and per diem employees are covered by the bloodborne pathogens standard. The ECP should describe how the standard will be met for these employees.

METHODS OF IMPLEMENTATION AND CONTROL

Universal Precautions

All employees will utilize universal precautions.

Exposure Control Plan

Employees covered by the bloodborne pathogens standard receive an explanation of this ECP during their initial training session. It will also be reviewed in their annual refresher training. All employees can review this plan at any time during their work shifts by contacting (Name of responsible person or department). If requested, we will provide an employee with a copy of the ECP free of charge and within 15 days of the request.

(Name of responsible person or department) is responsible for reviewing and updating the ECP annually or more frequently if necessary to reflect any new or modified tasks and procedures that affect occupational exposure and to reflect new or revised employee positions with occupational exposure.

Engineering Controls and Work Practices

Engineering controls and work practice controls will be used to prevent or minimize exposure to bloodborne pathogens. The

specific engineering controls and work practice controls used are listed below:

- (For example: non-glass capillary tubes, SESIPs, needleless systems)

- _____

- _____

Sharps disposal containers are inspected and maintained or replaced by (Name of responsible person or department) every (list frequency) or whenever necessary to prevent overfilling.

This facility identifies the need for changes in engineering controls and work practices through (Examples: Review of OSHA records, employee interviews, committee activities, etc.)

We evaluate new procedures and new products regularly by (Describe the process, literature reviewed, supplier info, products considered) _____.

Both front-line workers and management officials are involved in this process in the following manner: (Describe employees' involvement) _____

(Name of responsible person or department) is responsible for ensuring that these recommendations are implemented.

Personal Protective Equipment (PPE)

PPE is provided to our employees at no cost to them. Training in the use of the appropriate PPE for specific tasks or procedures is provided by (Name of responsible person or department).

The types of PPE available to employees are as follows: (gloves, eye protection, etc.) _____
_____
_____

PPE is located (List location) and may be obtained through (Name of responsible person or department). (Specify how employees will obtain PPE and who is responsible for ensuring that PPE is available.)

All employees using PPE must observe the following precautions:

- Wash hands immediately or as soon as feasible after removing gloves or other PPE.

- Remove PPE after it becomes contaminated and before leaving the work area.

- Used PPE may be disposed of in (List appropriate containers for storage, laundering, decontamination, or disposal.)

- Wear appropriate gloves when it is reasonably anticipated that there may be hand contact with blood or OPIM, and when handling or touching contaminated items or surfaces; replace gloves if torn, punctured or contaminated, or if their ability to function as a barrier is compromised.

- Utility gloves may be decontaminated for reuse if their integrity is not compromised; discard utility gloves if they show signs of cracking, peeling, tearing, puncturing, or deterioration.

- Never wash or decontaminate disposable gloves for reuse.

- Wear appropriate face and eye protection when splashes, sprays, spatters, or droplets of blood or OPIM pose a hazard to the eye, nose, or mouth.

- Remove immediately or as soon as feasible any garment contaminated by blood or OPIM, in such a way as to avoid contact with the outer surface.

The procedure for handling used PPE is as follows:
(may refer to specific procedure by title or number and last date of review; include how and where to decontaminate face shields, eye protection, resuscitation equipment)

Housekeeping

Regulated waste is placed in containers which are closable, constructed to contain all contents and prevent leakage, appropriately labeled or color-coded (see the following section "Labels"), and closed prior to removal to prevent spillage or protrusion of contents during handling.

The procedure for handling sharps disposal containers is: *(may refer to specific procedure by title or number and last date of review)*

_____

_____

The procedure for handling other regulated waste is: *(may refer to specific procedure by title or number and last date of review)*

_____

_____

Contaminated sharps are discarded immediately or as soon as possible in containers that are closable, puncture-resistant, leak proof on sides and bottoms, and appropriately labeled or color-coded. Sharps disposal containers are available at (must be easily accessible and as close as feasible to the immediate area where sharps are used).

Bins and pails (e.g., wash or emesis basins) are cleaned and decontaminated as soon as feasible after visible contamination.

Broken glassware that may be contaminated is only picked up using mechanical means, such as a brush and dustpan.

Laundry

The following contaminated articles will be laundered by this company:

_____

_____

Laundering will be performed by (Name of responsible person or department) at (time and/or location).

The following laundering requirements must be met:

▪ handle contaminated laundry as little as possible, with minimal agitation

▪ place wet contaminated laundry in leak-proof, labeled or color-coded containers before transport. Use (specify either red bags or bags marked with the biohazard symbol) for this purpose.

▪ wear the following PPE when handling and/or sorting contaminated laundry: (List appropriate PPE).

Labels

The following labeling methods are used in this facility:

Equipment to be Labeled   *Label Type (size, color)*

(specimens, contaminated laundry, etc.)   (red bag, biohazard label)

_____

(Name of responsible person or department) is responsible for ensuring that warning labels are affixed or red bags are used as required if regulated waste or contaminated equipment is brought into the facility. Employees are to notify (Name of responsible person or department) if they discover regulated waste containers, refrigerators containing blood or OPIM, contaminated equipment, etc., without proper labels.

HEPATITIS B VACCINATION

(Name of responsible person or department) will provide training to employees on hepatitis B vaccinations, addressing safety, benefits, efficacy, methods of administration, and availability.

The hepatitis B vaccination series is available at no cost after initial employee training and within 10 days of initial assignment to all employees identified in the exposure determination section of this plan. Vaccination is encouraged unless: 1) documentation exists that the employee has previously received the series; 2) antibody testing reveals that the employee is immune; or 3) medical evaluation shows that vaccination is contraindicated.

However, if an employee declines the vaccination, the employee must sign a declination form. Employees who decline may request and obtain the vaccination at a later date at no cost. Documentation of refusal of the vaccination is kept at (List location).

Vaccination will be provided by (List health care professional responsible for this part of the plan) at (location).

Following the medical evaluation, a copy of the health care professional's written opinion will be obtained and provided to the employee within 15 days of the completion of the evaluation. It will be limited to whether the employee requires the hepatitis vaccine and whether the vaccine was administered.

POST-EXPOSURE EVALUATION AND FOLLOW-UP

Should an exposure incident occur, contact (Name of responsible person) at the following number _____.

An immediately available confidential medical evaluation and follow-up will be conducted by (name of licensed health care professional). Following initial first aid (clean the wound, flush eyes or other mucous membrane, etc.), the following activities will be performed:

▪ Document the routes of exposure and how the exposure occurred.

▪ Identify and document the source individual (unless the employer can establish that identification is infeasible or prohibited by state or local law).

▪ Obtain consent and make arrangements to have the source individual tested as soon as possible to determine HIV, HCV, and HBV infectivity; document that the source individual's test results were conveyed to the employee's health care provider.

▪ If the source individual is already known to be HIV, HCV and/or HBV positive, new testing need not be performed.

▪ Assure that the exposed employee is provided with the source individual's test results and with information about applicable disclosure laws and regulations concerning the identity and infectious status of the source individual (e.g., laws protecting confidentiality).

▪ After obtaining consent, collect exposed employee's blood as soon as feasible after exposure incident, and test blood for HBV and HIV serological status

▪ If the employee does not give consent for HIV serological testing during collection of blood for baseline testing, preserve the baseline blood sample for at least 90 days; if the exposed employee elects to have the baseline sample tested during this waiting period, perform testing as soon as feasible.

ADMINISTRATION OF POST-EXPOSURE
EVALUATION AND FOLLOW-UP

(Name of responsible person or department) ensures that health care professional(s) responsible for employee's hepatitis B vaccination and post-exposure evaluation and follow-up are given a copy of OSHA's bloodborne pathogens standard.

(Name of responsible person or department) ensures that the health care professional evaluating an employee after an exposure incident receives the following:

- a description of the employee's job duties relevant to the exposure incident

- route(s) of exposure

- circumstances of exposure

- if possible, results of the source individual's blood test

- relevant employee medical records, including vaccination status

(Name of responsible person or department) provides the employee with a copy of the evaluating health care professional's written opinion within 15 days after completion of the evaluation.

PROCEDURES FOR EVALUATING THE CIRCUMSTANCES
SURROUNDING AN EXPOSURE INCIDENT

(Name of responsible person or department) will review the circumstances of all exposure incidents to determine:

- engineering controls in use at the time

- work practices followed

- a description of the device being used (including type and brand)

- protective equipment or clothing that was used at the time of the exposure incident (gloves, eye shields, etc.)

- location of the incident (O.R., E.R., patient room, etc.)

- procedure being performed when the incident occurred

- employee's training

(Name of Responsible Person) will record all percutaneous injuries from contaminated sharps in a Sharps Injury Log.

If revisions to this ECP are necessary (Responsible person or department) will ensure that appropriate changes are made. (Changes may include an evaluation of safer devices, adding employees to the exposure determination list, etc.)

EMPLOYEE TRAINING

All employees who have occupational exposure to bloodborne pathogens receive initial and annual training conducted by (Name of responsible person or department). (Attach a brief description of their qualifications.)

All employees who have occupational exposure to bloodborne pathogens receive training on the epidemiology, symptoms, and transmission of bloodborne pathogen diseases. In addition, the training program covers, at a minimum, the following elements:

- a copy and explanation of the OSHA bloodborne pathogen standard

- an explanation of our ECP and how to obtain a copy

- an explanation of methods to recognize tasks and other activities that may involve exposure to blood and OPIM, including what constitutes an exposure incident

- an explanation of the use and limitations of engineering controls, work practices, and PPE

- an explanation of the types, uses, location, removal, handling, decontamination, and disposal of PPE

- an explanation of the basis for PPE selection

- information on the hepatitis B vaccine, including information on its efficacy, safety, method of administration, the benefits of being vaccinated, and that the vaccine will be offered free of charge

- information on the appropriate actions to take and persons to contact in an emergency involving blood or OPIM

- an explanation of the procedure to follow if an exposure incident occurs, including the method of reporting the incident and the medical follow-up that will be made available

- information on the post-exposure evaluation and follow-up that the employer is required to provide for the employee following an exposure incident

- an explanation of the signs and labels and/or color coding required by the standard and used at this facility

- an opportunity for interactive questions and answers with the person conducting the training session.

Training materials for this facility are available at (name location).

RECORDKEEPING

Training Records

Training records are completed for each employee upon completion of training. These documents will be kept for at least three years at (Location of records).

The training records include:

- the dates of the training sessions

- the contents or a summary of the training sessions

- the names and qualifications of persons conducting the training

- the names and job titles of all persons attending the training sessions

Employee training records are provided upon request to the employee or the employee's authorized representative within 15 working days. Such requests should be addressed to (Name of responsible person or department).

Medical Records

Medical records are maintained for each employee with occupational exposure in accordance with 29 *CFR* 1910.1020, "Access to Employee Exposure and Medical Records."

(Name of Responsible person or department) is responsible for maintenance of the required medical records. These confidential records are kept in (List location) for at least the duration of employment plus 30 years.

Employee medical records are provided upon request of the employee or to anyone having written consent of the employee within 15 working days. Such requests should be sent to (Name of responsible person or department and address).

OSHA Recordkeeping

An exposure incident is evaluated to determine if the case meets OSHA's Recordkeeping Requirements (29 CFR 1904). This determination and the recording activities are done by (Name of responsible person or department).

Sharps Injury Log

In addition to the 1904 Recordkeeping Requirements, all percutaneous injuries from contaminated sharps are also recorded in a Sharps Injury Log. All incidences must include at least:

- date of the injury
- type and brand of the device involved (syringe, suture needle)
- department or work area where the incident occurred
- explanation of how the incident occurred.

This log is reviewed as part of the annual program evaluation and maintained for at least five years following the end of the calendar year covered. If a copy is requested by anyone, it must have any personal identifiers removed from the report.

HEPATITIS B VACCINE DECLINATION (MANDATORY)

I understand that due to my occupational exposure to blood or other potentially infectious materials I may be at risk of acquiring hepatitis B virus (HBV) infection. I have been given the opportunity to be vaccinated with hepatitis B vaccine, at no charge to myself. However, I decline hepatitis B vaccination at this time. I understand that by declining this vaccine, I continue to be at risk of acquiring hepatitis B, a serious disease. If in the future I continue to have occupational exposure to blood or other potentially infectious materials and I want to be vaccinated with hepatitis B vaccine, I can receive the vaccination series at no charge to me.

Signed: (Employee Name)   Date:

The hazard communication standard requires you to develop a written hazard communication program. The following is a sample hazard communication program that you may use as a guide in developing your program.

Part 2 Hazard Communication Standard

The following model Hazard Communication Program is based on the requirements of the OSHA Hazard Communications Standard, 29 CFR 1910.1200. The intent of this model is to provide an easy-to-use format to tailor to the specific requirements of your establishment.

Model Hazard Communication Program

1. Company Policy

To ensure that information about the dangers of all hazardous chemicals used by (Name of Company) is known by all affected employees, the following hazardous information program has been established. Under this program, you will be informed of the contents of the OSHA Hazard Communications standard, the hazardous properties of chemicals with which you work, safe handling procedures and measures to take to protect yourself from these chemicals.

This program applies to all work operations in our company where you may be exposed to hazardous chemicals under normal working conditions or during an emergency situation. All work units of this company will participate in the Hazard Communication Program. Copies of the Hazard Communication Program are available in the (location) for review by any interested employee.

(Name of responsible person and/or position) is the program coordinator, with overall responsibility for the program, including reviewing and updating this plan as necessary.

2. Container Labeling

(Name of responsible person and/or position) will verify that all containers received for use will be clearly labeled as to the contents, note the appropriate hazard warning, and list the manufacturer's name and address.

The (name of responsible person and/or position) in each section will ensure that all secondary containers are labeled with either an extra copy of the original manufacturer's label or with labels marked with the identity and the appropriate hazard warning. For help with labeling, see (name of responsible person and/or position).

On the following individual stationary process containers, we are using (description of labeling system used) rather than a label to convey the required information:

(List containers here).

We are using an in-house labeling system that relies on (describe any in-house system which uses numbers or graphics to convey hazard information).

The (name of responsible person and/or position) will review the company labeling procedures every (provide a time period) and will update labels as required.

3. Material Safety Data Sheets (MSDSs)

The (name of responsible person and/or position) is responsible for establishing and monitoring the company MSDS program. He/she will ensure that procedures are developed to obtain the necessary MSDSs and will review incoming MSDSs for new or significant health and safety information. He/she will see that any new information is communicated to affected employees. The procedure below will be followed when an MSDS is not received at the time of initial shipment:

(Describe procedure to be followed here)

Copies of MSDSs for all hazardous chemicals to which employees are exposed or are potentially exposed will be kept in (identify location).

MSDSs will be readily available to all employees during each work shift. If an MSDS is not available, contact (name of responsible person and/or position).

MSDSs will be readily available to employees in each work area using the following format:

(Describe company format here)

Note: If an alternative to paper copies of MSDSs is used, describe the format and how employees can access them.

When revised MSDSs are received, the following procedures will be followed to replace old MSDSs:

(Describe procedures)

4. Employee Training and Information

(Name of responsible person and/or position) is responsible for the Hazard Communication Program and will ensure that all program elements are carried out.

Everyone who works with or is potentially exposed to hazardous chemicals will receive initial training on the hazard communication standard and this plan before starting work. Each new employee will attend a health and safety orientation that includes the following information and training:

- An overview of the OSHA hazard communication standard
- The hazardous chemicals present at his/her work area
- The physical and health risks of the hazardous chemicals
- Symptoms of overexposure
- How to determine the presence or release of hazardous chemicals in the work area
- How to reduce or prevent exposure to hazardous chemicals through use of control procedures, work practices and personal protective equipment
- Steps the company has taken to reduce or prevent exposure to hazardous chemicals
- Procedures to follow if employees are overexposed to hazardous   chemicals
- How to read labels and MSDSs to obtain hazard information
- Location of the MSDS file and written Hazard Communication program

Prior to introducing a new chemical hazard into any section of this company, each employee in that section will be given information and training as outlined above for the new chemical hazard. The training format will be as follows:

(Describe training format, such as audiovisuals, interactive computer programs, classroom instruction, etc.)

5. Hazardous Non-routine Tasks

Periodically, employees are required to perform non-routine tasks that are hazardous. Examples of non-routine tasks are: confined space entry, tank cleaning, and painting reactor vessels.

Prior to starting work on such projects, each affected employee will be given information by (name of responsible person and/or position) about the hazardous chemicals he or she may encounter during such activity. This information will include specific chemical hazards, protective and safety measures the employee should use, and steps the company is taking to reduce the hazards, including ventilation, respirators, the presence of another employee (buddy systems), and emergency procedures.

Examples of non-routine tasks performed by employees of this company are:

Task	*Hazardous Chemical*
_____	_____
_____	_____
_____	_____
_____	_____

6. Informing Other Employers/Contractors

It is the responsibility of (Name of responsible person and/or position) to provide other employers and contractors with information about hazardous chemicals that their employees may be exposed to on a job site and suggested precautions for employees. It is the responsibility of (name of responsible person and/or position) to obtain information about hazardous chemicals used by other employers to which employees of this company may be exposed.

Other employers and contractors will be provided with MSDSs for hazardous chemicals generated by this company's operations in the following manner:

(Describe company policy here)

In addition to providing a copy of an MSDS to other employers, other employers will be informed of necessary precautionary measures to protect employees exposed to operations performed by this company.

Also, other employers will be informed of the hazard labels used by the company. If symbolic or numerical labeling systems are

used, the other employees will be provided with information to understand the labels used for hazardous chemicals for which their employees may have exposure.

7. List of Hazardous Chemicals

A list of all known hazardous chemicals used by our employees is attached to this plan. This list includes the name of the chemical, the manufacturer, the work area in which the chemical is used, dates of use, and quantity used. Further information on each chemical may be obtained from the MSDSs, located in (identify location).

When new chemicals are received, this list is updated (including date the chemicals were introduced) within 30 days. To ensure any new chemical is added in a timely manner, the following procedures shall be followed:

(Identify procedures to be followed)

The hazardous chemical inventory is compiled and maintained by (Name of responsible person and/or position and telephone number).

8. Chemicals in Unlabeled Pipes

Work activities are sometimes performed by employees in areas where chemicals are transferred through unlabeled pipes. Prior to starting work in these areas, the employee shall contact (name of responsible person and/or position) for information regarding:

- The chemical in the pipes
- Potential hazards
- Required safety precautions.

Include here the chemical list developed during the inventory. Arrange this list so that you are able to cross-reference it with your MSDS file and the labels on your containers. Additional useful information, such as the manufacturer's telephone number, an emergency number, scientific name, CAS number, the associated task, etc., can be included.

9. Program Availability

A copy of this program will be made available, upon request, to employees and their representatives.

OSHA assistance

OSHA can provide extensive help through a variety of programs, including technical assistance about effective safety and health programs, state plans, workplace consultations, voluntary protection programs, strategic partnerships, and training and education, and more. An overall commitment to workplace safety and health can add value to your business, to your workplace, and to your life.

Safety and health management system guidelines

Effective management of worker safety and health protection is a decisive factor in reducing the extent and severity of work-related injuries and illnesses and their related costs. In fact, an effective safety and health program forms the basis of good worker protection and can save time and money (about $4 for every dollar spent) and increase productivity and reduce worker injuries, illnesses, and related worker compensation costs.

To assist employers and employees in developing effective safety and health programs, OSHA published recommended Safety and Health Program Management Guidelines (Federal Register 54 (16): 3904-3916, January 26, 1989). These voluntary guidelines can be applied to all places of employment covered by OSHA.

The guidelines identify four general elements critical to the development of a successful safety and health management system:
- Management leadership and employee involvement.
- Workplace analysis.
- Hazard prevention and control.
- Safety and health training.

The guidelines recommend specific actions, under each of these general elements, to achieve an effective safety and health program. The Federal Register notice is available online at www.osha.gov.

State programs

There are 26 state plans and jurisdictions that operate their own occupational safety and health programs under plans approved by OSHA (23 cover both the private sector and state and local government employees, and three cover public employees only). These "state plan states" have standards which are identical to or at least as effective as federal OSHA standards, including the bloodborne pathogens and hazard communications standards. State plan states are required to extend their coverage to state and local government workers, including health care workers.

Additional information about state plans, and a list of those programs including contact information are available on OSHA's website.

OSHA consultation services

Consultation assistance is available on request to employers who want help in establishing and maintaining a safe and healthful workplace. Largely funded by OSHA, the service is provided at no cost to the employer. Primarily developed for smaller employers with more hazardous operations, the consultation service is delivered by state governments employing professional safety and health consultants. Comprehensive assistance includes an appraisal of all-mechanical systems, work practices, and occupational safety and health hazards of the workplace and all aspects of the employer's present job safety and health program. In addition, the service offers assistance to employers in developing and implementing an effective safety and health program. No penalties are proposed or citations issued for hazards identified by the consultant. OSHA provides consultation assistance to the employer with the assurance that his or her name and firm and any information about the workplace will not be routinely reported to OSHA enforcement staff.

Under the consultation program, certain exemplary employers may request participation in OSHA's Safety and Health Achievement Recognition Program (SHARP). Eligibility for participation in SHARP includes receiving a comprehensive consultation visit, demonstrating exemplary achievements in workplace safety

and health by abating all identified hazards, and developing an excellent safety and health program.

Employers accepted into SHARP may receive an exemption from programmed inspections (not complaint or accident investigation inspections) for a period of one year. For more information concerning consultation assistance, see the list of consultation projects listed at the end of this publication.

The OSHA Voluntary Protection Program (VPP)

Voluntary Protection Programs and onsite consultation services, when coupled with an effective enforcement program, expand worker protection to help meet the goals of the OSH Act. The three VPP program levels include Star, Merit, and Demonstration and are designed to recognize outstanding achievements by companies that have successfully incorporated comprehensive safety and health programs into their total management system. The VPP motivate others to achieve excellent safety and health results in the same outstanding way as they establish a cooperative relationship between employers, employees, and OSHA.

For additional information on VPP and how to apply, contact the OSHA regional offices listed at the end of this publication.

Strategic Partnership Programs

OSHA's Strategic Partnership Program, the newest member of OSHA's cooperative programs, helps encourage, assist, and recognize the efforts of partners to eliminate serious workplace hazards and achieve a high level of worker safety and health. Whereas OSHA's Consultation Program and VPP entail one-on-one relationships between OSHA and individual work sites, most strategic partnerships seek to have a broader impact by building cooperative relationships with groups of employers and employees. These partnerships are voluntary, cooperative relationships between OSHA, employers, employee representatives, and others (e.g., trade unions, trade and professional associations, universities, and other government agencies).

For more information on this and other cooperative programs, contact your nearest OSHA office, or visit www.osha.gov.

The OSHA Alliance Program

Alliances enable organizations committed to workplace safety and health to collaborate with OSHA to prevent injuries and illnesses in the workplace. OSHA and its allies work together to reach out to, educate, and lead the nation's employers and their employees in improving and advancing workplace safety and health.

Alliances are open to all, including trade or professional organizations, businesses, labor organizations, educational institutions, and government agencies. In some cases, organizations may be building on existing relationships with OSHA through other cooperative programs.

There are few formal program requirements for alliances, which are less structured than other cooperative agreements, and the agreements do not include an enforcement component. However, OSHA and the participating organizations must define, implement, and meet a set of short- and long-term goals that fall into three categories: training and education; outreach and communication; and promotion of the national dialogue on workplace safety and health.

OSHA training and education

OSHA area offices offer a variety of information services, such as compliance assistance, technical advice, publications, audiovisual aids and speakers for special engagements. OSHA's Training Institute in Des Plaines, IL, provides basic and advanced courses in safety and health for federal and state compliance officers, state consultants, federal agency personnel, and private sector employers, employees, and their representatives.

The OSHA Training Institute also has established OSHA Training Institute Education Centers to address the increased demand for its courses from the private sector and from other federal agencies. These centers are nonprofit colleges, universities, and other organizations that have been selected after a competition for participation in the program.

OSHA also provides funds to nonprofit organizations, through grants, to conduct workplace training and education in subjects where OSHA believes there is a lack of workplace training. Grants are awarded annually. Grant recipients are expected to contribute 20 percent of the total grant cost.

For more information on grants, training, and education, contact the OSHA Training Institute, Office of Training and Education, 1555 Times Drive, Des Plaines, IL 60018, (847) 297-4810. For further information on any OSHA program, contact your nearest OSHA area or regional office listed at the end of this publication.

Information available electronically

OSHA has a variety of materials and tools available on its website at www.osha.gov. These include e-Tools such as Expert Advisors, Electronic Compliance Assistance Tools (e-cats), Technical Links; regulations, directives, publications; videos, and other information for employers and employees. OSHA's software programs and compliance assistance tools walk you through challenging safety and health issues and common problems to find the best solutions for your workplace.

OSHA publications

OSHA has an extensive publications program. For a listing of free or sales items, visit OSHA's website at www.osha.gov or contact the OSHA Publications Office, U.S. Department of Labor, 200 Constitution Avenue NW, N-3101, Washington, DC 20210. Telephone (202) 693-1888 or fax to (202) 693-2498.

Contacting OSHA

To report an emergency, file a complaint, or seek OSHA advice, assistance, or products, call (800) 321-OSHA or contact your nearest OSHA regional or area office listed at the end of this publication. The teletypewriter (TTY) number is (877) 889-5627.

You can also file a complaint online and obtain more information on OSHA federal and state programs by visiting OSHA's website at www.osha.gov.

For more information on grants, training, and education, contact the OSHA Training Institute, Office of Training and Education, 1555 Times Drive, Des Plaines, IL 60018, (847) 297-4810, or see Outreach on OSHA's website at www.osha.gov.

OSHA Regional Offices

Region I
(CT,* ME, MA, NH, RI, VT*)
Boston, MA 02203
(617) 565-9860

Region II
(NJ,* NY,* PR,* VI*)
201 Varick Street, Room 670
New York, NY 10014
(212) 337-2378

Region III
(DE, DC, MD,* PA,* VA,* WV)
The Curtis Center
170 S. Independence Mall West
Suite 740 West
Philadelphia, PA 19106-3309
(215) 861-4900

Region IV
(AL, FL, GA, KY,* MS, NC,* SC,* TN*)
Atlanta Federal Center
61 Forsyth Street SW, Room 6T50
Atlanta, GA 30303
(404) 562-2300

Region V
(IL, IN,* MI,* MN,* OH, WI)
230 South Dearborn Street, Room 3244
Chicago, IL 60604
(312) 353-2220

Region VI
(AR, LA, NM,* OK, TX)
525 Griffin Street, Room 602
Dallas, TX 75202
(214) 767-4731 or 4736 x224

Region VII
(IA,* KS, MO, NE)
City Center Square
1100 Main Street, Suite 800
Kansas City, MO 64105
(816) 426-5861

Region VIII
(CO, MT, ND, SD, UT,* WY*)
1999 Broadway, Suite 1690
PO Box 46550
Denver, CO 80202-5716
(303) 844-1600

Region IX
(American Samoa, AZ,* CA,* HI, NV,* Northern Mariana Islands)
71 Stevenson Street, Room 420
San Francisco, CA 94105
(415) 975-4310

Region X
(AK,* ID, OR,* WA*)
1111 Third Avenue, Suite 715
Seattle, WA 98101-3212
(206) 553-5930

*These states and territories operate their own OSHA-approved job safety and health programs (Connecticut, New Jersey, and New York plans cover public employees only). States with approved programs must have a standard that is identical to, or at least as effective as, the federal standard.

Note: To get contact information for OSHA Area Offices, OSHA-approved state plans, and OSHA Consultation Projects, please visit us online at www.osha.gov or call us at (800) 321-OSHA.

www.ingramcontent.com/pod-product-compliance
Lightning Source LLC
Chambersburg PA
CBHW051828170526
45167CB00005B/2204